# THE FRENCH REVOLUTION

## People Power in Action
## History 5th Grade
## Children's European History

Speedy Publishing LLC
40 E. Main St. #1156
Newark, DE 19711
www.speedypublishing.com

The French Revolution led to huge changes not just in France, but in countries all around the world. It was and is an inspiration to people's movements for reform and power-sharing. Read on and learn why and how the French Revolution happened!

# RADICAL CHANGE

In the French Revolution, a popular uprising overthrew the government of the French king and took control of the country.

NAPOLEON BONAPARTE

The Revolution began in 1789 and lasted until 1799. It started with revolutionaries attacking the Bastille, a prison, and letting out the prisoners. It ended when a general, Napoleon Bonaparte, threw out the revolutionary government and made himself the leader of France.

During the Revolution, French citizens overturned the way France had been governed for hundreds of years. They got rid of the absolute power of the king and much of the power of the nobility and of the Roman Catholic Church. The changes opened the way for new thoughts, new ways of living, new ways of doing business, and new hopes.

NAPOLEON BONAPARTE AT THE BATTLE OF RIVOLI

The Revolution was not all smooth progress. It was often chaotic, often violent, and often did not come close to doing everything it hoped to do. But it still brought forward ideas such as government needing the consent of those it governs, and basic human rights like freedom and life itself. It showed what people, even poor people, can accomplish when they join together.

Before the Revolution, the king ruled with almost absolute power. The people of France were divided into "estates". The First Estate were the leaders and priests of the Roman Catholic Church. The Second Estate were the nobility. The Third Estate were the commoners, by far the largest number of people, and the group with the smallest amount of power.

People of the Third Estate provided most of the income for the Second Estate through taxes, and the Second Estate spent it on living, well, like kings. Because of bad choices, huge spending, and an expensive war, France was nearly bankrupt. There had also been a drought and poor harvests that drove up the price of bread and basic foods, and caused the Third Estate to be very unhappy. There were riots, strikes, and theft of grain supplies.

In 1786 the government decided to extend the land tax to include the Second Estate, to raise enough money to run the government. The nobles were strongly opposed to paying any taxes. King Louis XVI decided to call the three Estates into an assembly. He wanted to gain support for the new taxes, but also agreed to hear complaints that the three Estates would submit.

KING LOUIS XVI

BATTLE OF VAROUX IN FRENCH REVOLUTION

# THE THIRD ESTATE RISES

The Third Estate was over 98% of the population of France, but in the Estates-General the other two bodies could out-vote the Third Estate. People started calling for the end of veto power for the nobles and clergy: they wanted representative voting.

All three Estates wanted general reform of the government, the courts, and finances, but the nobles were strongly opposed to giving up any of their power. By the summer of 1789 the three Estates could not agree on enough to allow the meeting to go forward. So the Third Estate decided to have its own meeting!

The Third Estate renamed itself the National Assembly and vowed to continue meeting until France had a new constitution and a new way of governing itself. A week later most of the clergy and some of the nobles joined the National Assembly, and soon after the king accepted the new body.

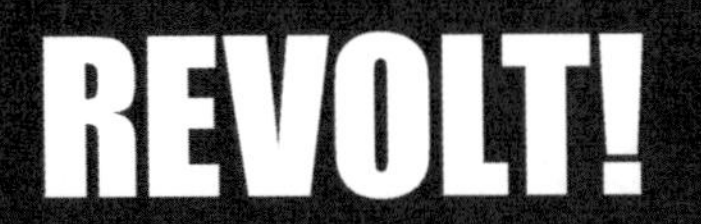


While the National Assembly worked on a constitution, tensions continued to rise throughout the country. People in Paris began to hear rumors that the army was going to dissolve the National Assembly and take over the country.

NATIONAL ASSEMBLY

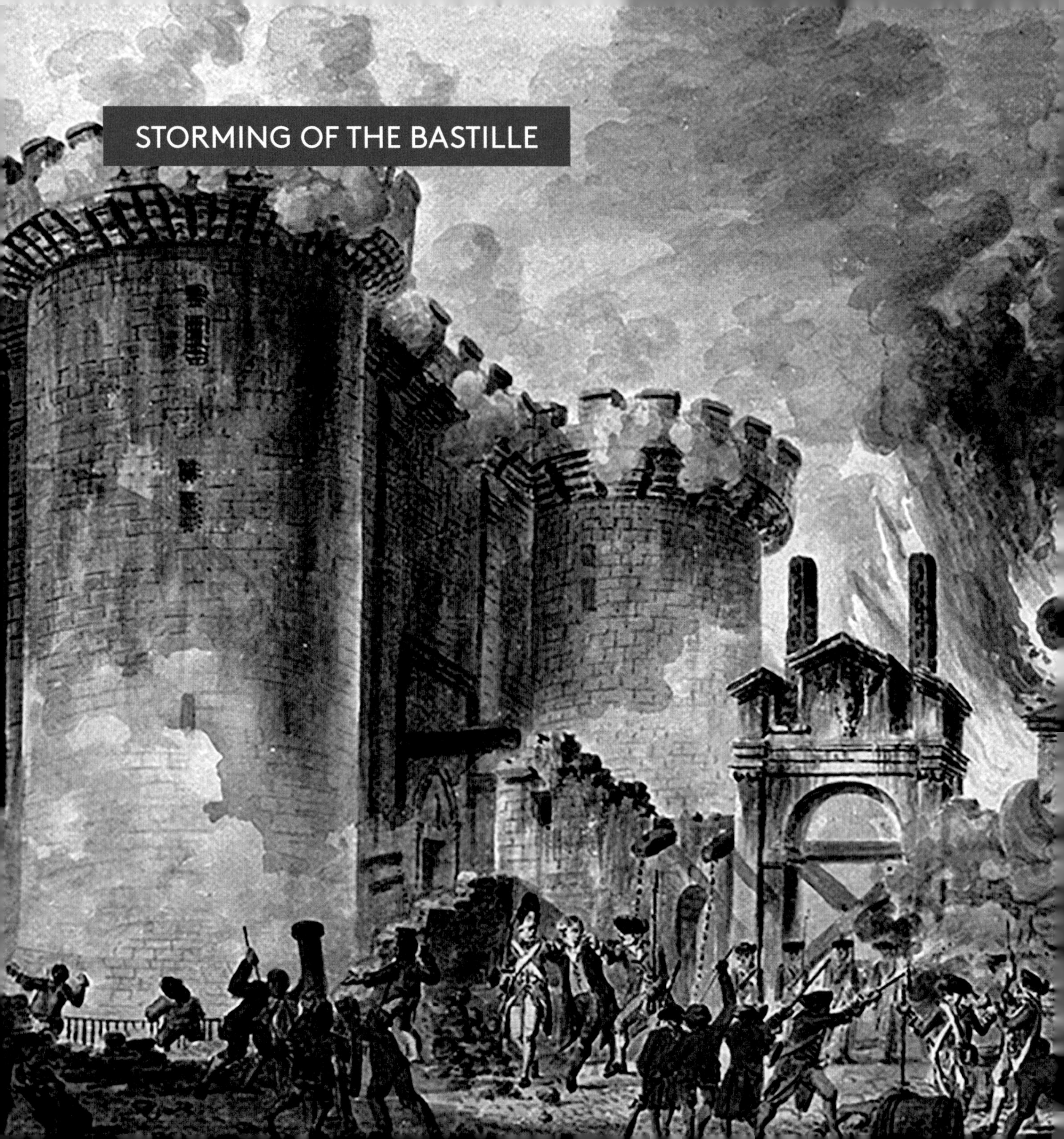

STORMING OF THE BASTILLE

In response, on July 14, a mob of people attacked the Bastille fortress and prison in Paris. They wanted to free prisoners and to get weapons with which to resist if the army attacked. In France, July 14 is Bastille Day, a national holiday that marks the start of the French Revolution.

A wave of fear and violence, known as The Great Fear, spread out from Paris. Mobs broke into the homes of nobles, landlords, and tax collectors, taking what they could find and burning the houses. The National Assembly signed a law in August of 1789 that ended feudalism, the system under which the nobles basically owned everything, including the people who worked on their land.

# THE RIGHTS OF MAN

Also in August, the Assembly passed the Declaration of the Rights of Man and the Citizen. This document stated the Assembly's goal of replacing the old government and system of power with a new system. Key "rights" were freedom of speech, equal opportunity, and representative government.

The Assembly was very slow in putting its constitution together. They argued for a long time about who would have the right to elect delegates to future National Assemblies, if the clergy were to be loyal to the Pope or the French government, and how much power the king should continue to have.

Their task was not completed until 1791. France's first written constitution established a constitutional monarchy, in which the king could appoint the chief ministers and veto bills. Radical members of the Assembly were not happy with this moderate constitution, and began to campaign for more changes. They also wanted to put the king on trial for crimes against the people.

Chief among the radicals were Maximilien de Robespierre, Camille Desmoulins, and Georges Danton. They were part of an extremist group known as the Jacobins. Learn more about them in the Baby Professor book, They Got Involved!

JACOBIN CLUB
SOCIÉTÉ DES JACOBINS

## GOOD INTENTIONS TURN BAD

Under the new constitution, elections were held for a new Legislative Assembly. The Assembly worried that Austria and Prussia were planning to attack France and overthrow the revolution, so it declared war on those two countries in 1792. The Assembly also wanted to spread its new ideas of how countries should be governed.

At the same time, tensions inside France were growing steadily higher. In August, 1792, a mob led by Jacobins attacked the king's residence in Paris and arrested the king. Violence kept mounting, with different parties fighting each other over who was more true to the revolution. Hundreds of people were killed in street battles. In September, 1792, a National Convention replaced the Legislative Assembly. The convention declared a French republic, and said that the monarchy was abolished.

EXECUTION OF LOUIS XVI

# THE KING DIES

In 1793 the National Convention found King Louis XVI guilty of crimes against the nation and sentenced him to death. He was executed with the guillotine, a device with a huge sliding blade that cut off the condemned person's head.

Executions were done in public, and large crowds turned out as thousands of nobles, clergy, and supposed traitors went to the guillotine. The Queen, Marie-Antoinette was among them, and was executed nine months after her husband.

QUEEN MARIE ANTOINETTE LED TO HER EXECUTION

NAPOLEON BONAPARTE LEADING HIS TROOPS OVER THE BRIDGE OF ARCOLE

From the death of the king, the revolution became more and more violent. In June, 1793 the Jacobins took control of the National Convention. They declared the end of Christianity and even created a new calendar with new names for all the months!

On a more serious note, under the Jacobins there was a ten-month-long "reign of terror", when thousands of supposed "enemies of the revolution" were sent to the guillotine. Robespierre was the head of the "Committee of Public Safety" and ordered many of the executions.

COMMITTEE OF PUBLIC SAFETY

EXECUTION OF ROBESPIERRE

People finally rebelled against the actions of the Jacobins and the wave of violence. Robespierre himself was executed by guillotine in July, 1794. Over 17,000 people were officially executed during this time, and many more died in prison.

# THE END OF THE REVOLUTION

In 1795 the survivors of the Reign of Terror approved a new constitution. Now France would be led by a parliament and five "Directors". The nobles and the Jacobins objected to this plan, but the army, under the heroic general Napoleon Bonaparte, supported the Directory.

NATIONAL CONVENTION ON 9 THERMIDOR, 1794

NAPOLEON BONAPARTE AS THE 1ST CONSUL

The Directory was neither good at its job nor popular. It relied more and more on the support of the army. Finally, Bonaparte felt that enough was enough. He abolished the Directory and appointed himself "consul" and sole leader of France.

This was the end of the French Revolution, although many of its reforms continued, and the start of the Napoleonic Era.

# THE INFLUENCE OF THE FRENCH REVOLUTION

The French Revolution brought in a new political and social structure for the nation. It ended the power of the French royal family, ended the feudal system where the people who worked the land were basically the property of the dukes and counts. It opened the way for new ideas such as the end of slavery, equal rights for women, and equal opportunity for all. It took a long time for some of these ideas to become reality. But they started in the French Revolution.

# MARCH INTO THE FRENCH REVOLUTION

There is much more to learn about the French Revolution! Read Baby Professor books like Marie Antoinette and her Lavish Parties, Moms Need Bread!, and Are You With Us or Against Us? to find out more.

Visit
BABY PROFESSOR
EDUCATION KIDS
www.BabyProfessorBooks.com
to download Free Baby Professor eBooks
and view our catalog of new and exciting
Children's Books

Made in the USA
Middletown, DE
02 April 2020